CRICKET

NUMBER

CRICKET QUIZ BOOK

NUMBER ONE

by

R. A. GOODCHILD

JOHN GOODCHILD, PUBLISHERS
70 CARRINGTON CRESCENT, WENDOVER,
BUCKINGHAMSHIRE
TELEPHONE: WENDOVER (0296) 623646

First published April 1978

COVER DESIGN AND ILLUSTRATIONS

IAN MACKINTOSH

CONDITIONS OF SALE. This book is sold subject to the condition that it shall not, by way of trade or otherwise, be lent, resold, hired out or otherwise circulated without the publisher's prior consent in any form of binding or cover other than that in which it is published and without a similar condition including this condition being imposed on the subsequent purchaser.

© R. A. GOODCHILD 1977

ISBN 0 903445 28 X

PRINTED IN GREAT BRITAIN BY
R. J. ACFORD LTD.,
CHICHESTER, SUSSEX

CONTENTS

Page
- 7 The Field of Play
- 8 Scoring
- 9 Some Cricket Terms
- 10 The County Championship
- 11 One-Day Matches
- 12 Some County Records
- 13 Some Strange Records
- 14 A family Affair
- 15 All Round the World
- 16 Back Home Again
- 17 Some Nicknames
- 18 Some Great Batsmen
- 19 Some Great Bowlers
- 20 All-Rounders
- 21 'Twins'
- 22 Delving Into History
- 23 Test Cricket
- 24 England and Australia
- 25 The West Indies
- 26 India
- 27 Pakistan
- 28 South Africa
- 29 New Zealand
- 30 Not so Well Known

THE FIELD OF PLAY

1. How many players are there in a cricket team?
2. What is a wicket?
3. How long is the pitch?
4. How high are the stumps?
5. How wide may a bat be?
6. Where are (a) the bowling crease? (b) the popping crease? (c) the return crease?
7. How often may the pitch be rolled during a match?
8. What is a cricket ball made of?
9. A new ball may be taken at the start of each innings, and after 85 overs have been bowled during an innings. Can the ball be changed at any other time during a match?
10. All the cricket balls made in England are made in one county. Which one?

(Answers on Page 31)

SCORING

1. How are runs scored?

2. What is an overthrow?

3. For what offences can a bowler be no-balled?

4. What is a bye?

5. How does the umpire signal (a) a no-ball? (b) a boundary?

6. Can a batsman be out from a no-ball? If so, how?

7. Runs can only be scored when the ball is in play; the batsman cannot score and cannot be given out when the ball is 'dead'. When *is* the ball dead?

8. How does the umpire signal (a) a wide? (b) a leg-bye?

9. What is the difference between a draw and a tie?

10. The result of a game may be expressed in two ways. One is by the difference in the number of runs the sides have scored, i.e. 'Surrey won by 32 runs'. What is the other way?

(Answers on Pages 31 and 32)

SOME CRICKET TERMS

1. What is a hat-trick?
2. What is meant by (a) Round the wicket? (b) Over the wicket?
3. What is a googly?
4. What is a full toss?
5. What are 'extras'?
6. To a right-hander, which side is the 'off'?
7. What is meant by 'a maiden'?
8. What is a 'follow-on'?
9. What is a stonewaller?
10. What is a lob?

(Answers on Pages 32 and 33)

THE COUNTY CHAMPIONSHIP

1. How many county teams are there in the County Championships?

2. Which county has won the Championship the greatest number of times?

3. Which county won the Championship seven times running? And when?

4. Which county was once in the Championship, but is now a Minor County?

5. Who scored the fastest ever century in the Championship?

6. Which was the last county to join the Championship?

7. Which County Cricket Club was formed in 1789, joined the Championship in 1895, but did not win the Championship until 1975?

8. How are points awarded in the Championship?

9. How are bonus points for batting awarded?

10. How are bonus points for bowling awarded?

(Answers on Pages 33 and 34)

ONE-DAY MATCHES

1. In the Gillette Cup Competition, how many overs may be bowled in each innings?

2. Into how many zones are teams divided in the Benson and Hedges Cup Competition?

3. Which countries competed for the Prudential World Cup in 1975?

4. How many overs may a bowler bowl in an innings in (a) The Gillette Cup? (b) The John Player League? (c) The Benson and Hedges Cup?

5. Which team won the Prudential World Cup in 1975?

6. What is the greatest number of sixes hit in one season in the John Player League Competition?

7. What is the lowest score made by a team in the Gillette Cup Competition?

8. What is the highest score made by a team in the Benson and Hedges Cup Competition?

9. What is the highest score made by a batsman in the John Player League Competition?

10. What is the best bowling analysis in the Gillette Cup Competition?

(Answers on Page 34)

SOME COUNTY RECORDS

1. What is the greatest number of runs scored off one six-ball over? Who scored it?

2. What is the highest total made in an innings in the County Championship? Which county made it?

3. What is the lowest score for an innings in the Championship? Which county made it?

4. What is the highest score made by a batsman in the Championship? Who made it?

5. What is the highest batting average achieved by an English batsman in a season? Who was the batsman?

6. What is the greatest number of catches made during a Championship match? Who caught them all?

7. What is the highest score for the 1st wicket made in the Championship, and who made it?

8. What is the greatest number of wickets taken in a season? Who took them?

9. What is the greatest number of centuries scored in a season? Who made them?

10. What is the greatest number of catches made in a Championship match by a wicket-keeper? Who was he?

(Answers on Pages 34 and 35)

SOME STRANGE RECORDS

1. Eight cricketers have played in Test Matches both *for* England and *against* England. Name as many of them as you can.

2. One man played rugger *for* England and cricket *against* England. Who was he?

3. What is the lowest total made in an innings in a Test Match? Who made it?

4. In which game between an English team and a team from abroad were (a) over 1300 runs scored in three days for the loss of only 7 wickets: (b) the side batting first scored 343 for the 1st wicket; (c) in the side batting second one batsman scored over 300?

5. Two Test Matches were left unfinished because English teams had to leave to catch a boat. Where, and between whom, were they played?

6. In which match did a team lose by 2 runs because a bowler in the other team did the hat-trick and took the last three wickets? Who was the bowler?

7. What was the slowest bit of batting ever by an English player in a Test Match?

(Answers on Page 35)

A FAMILY AFFAIR

1. Two brothers played for South Africa in all four Test Matches against Australia in 1970. Who were they?

2. In 1931 a father and son played in the same team in the County Cricket Championship, and both made centuries in the same innings. Who were they, and which county did they play for?

3. Two brothers, playing for the same county, both scored two separate hundreds in the same match. Who were they, and which county did they play for?

4. In a Test Match at Lords in 1966 two cousins put up a record score for the 6th wicket. Who were they, and which team did they play for?

5. Three brothers played for England in the same Test Match. Who were they?

6. Two brothers, going in first for Somerset, made over 100 runs together three times running. Who were they?

7. What is the greatest number of brothers to play for the same English county?

8. Four brothers have all played in Tests for Pakistan, and three of them have played in the same match. Name all four if you can.

9. In 1972 two brothers each scored a century in the same innings in a Test Match. Who were they?

10. Only four cricketers have managed to score a century and then take all ten wickets in an innings, in one match, but two brothers have managed this feat—not, of course, in the same match. Can you name the brothers?

(Answers on Page 36)

ALL ROUND THE WORLD

1. In which European countries, outside Great Britain, is cricket played?

2. In which Asian countries, excluding India and Pakistan, is cricket played?

3. For what are the following trophies presented: (a) The Shell Shield? (b) The Plunket Cup? (c) The Wisden Trophy? (d) The Lawrence Trophy?

4. In 1956 New Zealand scored its first victory in a Test Match. Whom did it beat?

5. Where are the following cricket grounds: (a) Sabina Park? (b) Fenners? (c) Basin Reserve?

6. Three Indian cricketers have played Test cricket for England, and all three scored a century in their first Test Match. Who were they, where did they play their first Test, and when?

7. The records for the greatest number of runs made in Test Matches, and the greatest number of wickets taken in Tests, are both held by cricketers from the same country. Who are the cricketers, and what team did they play for?

8. Which Test teams made (a) the greatest number of runs in one day in a Test Match? (b) the lowest score in a day in a Test?

9. In 1877 Australia beat England in the first Test Match by 45 runs. What was the result of the Centenary Test in Australia in 1977?

10. Who were the Captains of the two Test teams in the Centenary Test, and where was the game played?

(Answers on Pages 36 and 37)

BACK HOME AGAIN

1. Who was the last batsman to score 1000 runs before the end of May?

2. What is the highest score made by an English schoolboy?

3. Which bowler did the hat-trick by having three batsmen stumped off his bowling?

4. Which batsman hit the greatest number of sixes in a match, and how many did he hit?

5. What is the highest score made by a batsman in Tests in England, and who made it?

6. What is the greatest number of wickets taken in a Test Match by a bowler? Who was the bowler, and what team was he playing against?

7. Which county managed to win a game in the Championship without losing a wicket?

8. What is the highest score made by a batsman in an Oxford v Cambridge cricket match? Who made it?

9. What is the lowest total made in an Oxford v Cambridge match?

(Answers on Pages 37 and 38)

SOME NICKNAMES

We give you the nickname and a few clues; you guess who they are.

1. THE DON. He captained Australia and made nineteen centuries against England, including one score of over 300.

2. THE GUV'NOR. He captained England. He made the highest score ever made by a Gloucestershire batsman, and in one County game he took 17 wickets.

3. THE DEMON. He played for Australia and took fourteen English wickets in one match, and did the hat-trick in another.

4. FIERY FRED. He played for Yorkshire and England, and took more wickets in Test Matches than any other fast bowler.

5. TIGER. He played for New South Wales and Australia and took more than 100 wickets in Test Matches against England. He and the Don shared a record 9th wicket partnership against South Africa.

6. TYPHOON. He played for Northamptonshire and England, and took 76 wickets in only seventeen Tests.

(Answers on Page 38)

SOME GREAT BATSMEN

1. Which cricketer played for Oxford, Middlesex and England, and scored 466 not out at the age of eighteen?

2. What is the highest individual score made in first class cricket, and who made it?

3. What is the highest individual score made by a batsman in first class cricket in: (a) Australia? (b) India? (c) New Zealand? (d) The West Indies? In each case, name the batsman if you can.

4. Which two cricketers scored over 1000 runs in a season 28 times?

5. Which great batsman scored over 61,000 runs and made 197 centuries in first class cricket?

6. What was the greatest number of runs scored in a day by a batsman, and who was the batsman?

7. Which two players, both members of the same team, scored over 3000 runs in the same season? Names and team, please.

8. What is the highest total made by a team in first class cricket, and which team made it?

9. Which cricketer made over 50,000 runs and over 150 centuries, and scored two centuries in the same match on seven occasions?

10. Who made the highest score for an English touring side in Australia, and how many did he score?

(Answers on Pages 38 and 39)

SOME GREAT BOWLERS

1. Who took all ten wickets in an innings twice in a season against the same team? Against which team?

2. In one game a bowler did the hat-trick and also took four wickets with four balls. Who was the bowler, and against which team was he playing?

3. Playing for his county, a bowler took 10 for 10, 9 for 12 and 7 for 9. Who was the bowler? Which county did he play for? And against which sides did he perform those feats?

4. Which bowler took over 4000 wickets in his career, and took 100 wickets in a season on twenty three occasions?

5. Which three English bowlers have taken over 250 wickets in Tests?

6. Which two West Indian bowlers have taken over 250 wickets in Tests?

7. Which four Australian bowlers have taken over 200 wickets in Tests?

8. Which two New Zealand bowlers have taken over 100 wickets in Tests?

9. Which two Pakistan bowlers have taken over 100 wickets in Tests?

10. Which Australian bowler did the hat-trick twice in one afternoon in a Test?

(Answers on Page 39)

ALL-ROUNDERS

1. What is 'the double'? When was it last done, and by whom?

2. Who did 'the double' the most times in his career?

3. Who took part in a record 1st wicket partnership for England against Australia *and* a record 10th wicket partnership?

4. Who is the only Australian player to have scored over 2000 runs and taken over 200 wickets in Test cricket?

5. Which Indian cricketer took part in the highest 1st. wicket partnership in Test cricket, and twice took eight wickets in an innings in Test matches?

6. Which Middlesex and England player has taken over 2000 wickets in his career, and scored over 20,000 runs?

7. Which South African cricketer scored over 2500 runs in Test cricket, and took over 100 wickets?

8. Who played for England at cricket and football, played in an F.A. Cup Final, and held the World Record for Long Jump?

(Answers on Pages 39 and 40)

'TWINS'

Sometimes we always think of cricketers in pairs; i.e. of two batsmen who opened for England or Australia or for a county, or of two fast bowlers who played in the same team.
Here you will find the name of one man, and you must think of the man you associate with him.

1. Hutton and . . . . . . went in first for England.

2. Simpson and . . . . . . went in first for Australia.

3. Lock and . . . . . . bowled for Surrey and England.

4. Miller and . . . . . . bowled for Australia.

5. Ramadhin and . . . . were great spin-bowlers for the West Indies.

6. Compton and . . . . played for Middlesex and England.

7. Hobbs and . . . . . . made over 100 for the 1st wicket fifteen times in Tests.

8. Trueman and . . . . both took over 250 wickets in Tests.

10. Lillee and . . . . bowled for Australia.

(Answers on Pages 40 and 41)

DELVING INTO HISTORY

1. Where is the oldest cricket-bat in the world?

2. Which great poet played for Harrow against Eton in 1805?

3. What series of games, which began in 1806, came to an end in 1962?

4. What are the two oldest series of cricket matches still being played?

5. What was the first match of which we know the full score?

6. Who scored a century playing in his 100th Test for England, and when did this happen?

7. When was Lord's cricket ground opened at St. John's Wood?

8. Where, and when, was the first century in Test cricket scored? Who scored it?

9. In 1796 all the members of a school cricket team were flogged by their Headmaster after playing in the first school match on record. What school did the victims attend, and against whom had they played?

(Answers on Page 41)

TEST CRICKET

1. What are the Ashes? What was their origin, and when did England last win them?

2. Between which two countries was the first Test Match played, and who won?

3. Name the six countries against which England has played Test Matches?

4. In which Test series were both sides captained by players who were both captains of the same county? Who were the captains, and which county did they captain?

5. Which bowler took the greatest number of wickets in a Test series? How many did he take, and against which country?

6. Which country won its first Test series in 1969? Which country did it beat?

7. In the whole history of Test cricket there has been only one tie. When did this happen, and between which teams?

8. Which Test teams were captained by: (a) G.S. Chappell? (b) A. Bacher? (c) Intikhab Alam? (d) C.H. Lloyd? (e) A.W. Greig? (f) B.S. Bedi?

9. On only four occasions has a team won a Test series 5–0. When was this done, and between which teams?

10. Four batsmen have scored a century and a double-century in the same Test match. Who were they, for whom were they playing, and against whom were they playing?

(Answers on Page 42)

ENGLAND AND AUSTRALIA

1. In 1971 England regained the Ashes, and won a Test series against Australia for the first time since 1956. Who captained England in 1970–71, and who captained Australia?

2. In 1968 M.C. Cowdrey captained England and W.M. Lawry captained Australia, but in one Test Match neither of them played. Who were the captains in this Test, and where was it played?

3. What was the heaviest defeat suffered by either side?

4. In 1902 two of the closest results in Test cricket occurred, one a win for Australia, and the other a win for England. Where were the games played, and what was the margin of victory in each case?

5. Two batsmen scored the greatest number of centuries and the greatest number of runs for their respective countries. Who were they and how many centuries did they score?

6. What was the greatest number of wickets taken by a bowler in one Test Match, and where did this happen?

7. What is the greatest number of centuries scored in one Test Match?

(Answers on Pages 42 and 43)

THE WEST INDIES

1. The West Indies play Tests against five other countries. Which West Indian batsmen have scored centuries against all five?

2. Two West Indian batsmen have made over 300 runs in a Test innings. Who are they, and against which teams were they playing?

3. Which West Indian bowler has taken 12 wickets in a Test Match, and against which country?

4. What is the lowest score made by a West Indian team in a Test Match, and against whom was it made?

5. What is the lowest score made against the West Indies in a Test Match, and who made it?

6. What is the largest score made against the West Indies in a Test Match, and who made it?

7. Two West Indian bowlers have taken eight wickets in an innings in a Test Match. Who are they?

8. Two West Indian bowlers have done the hat-trick in Test Matches. Who are they, and against whom did they do it?

9. A West Indian bowled the greatest number of balls in one Test Match. Who was he, and how many balls did he bowl?

10. What is the greatest number of batsmen in a Test series dismissed by a West Indian wicket-keeper? And who was he?

(Answers on Pages 43 and 44)

INDIA

1. Only two Indian batsmen have scored two separate centuries in a Test Match. Who were they, and against whom did they perform this feat?

2. Four Indian batsmen have scored double-centuries in Tests. Who are they?

3. What is the highest score made by India in Test Matches, and against whom was it scored?

4. What is the lowest score made in Tests by India, and against whom was it made?

5. What was the highest partnership in a match in India and which two batsmen achieved it? (It was also the highest in first class cricket anywhere in the world.)

6. Two Indian batsmen put up a record for the opening partnership in Test cricket. Who were they, what did they score, and which country were they playing against?

7. Two Indian bowlers have taken 9 wickets in one innings in a Test Match. Who are they, and against which countries did they achieve that feat?

8. One Indian bowler took 14 wickets in one Test Match. Who was he, and what team was he bowling to?

9. In 1977 England won a Test series in India for the first time since 1933–4. Who captained England, and who captained India?

10. Three Indians have scored over 3000 runs in Test cricket. Names, please.

(Answers on Page 44)

PAKISTAN

1. Only one Pakistan batsman has scored over 3000 runs in Test cricket. Who is he?

2. Four Pakistan batsmen have made double-centuries in Tests. Who are they, and against whom did they achieve that feat?

3. What is the highest score made by Pakistan in a Test Match? Against whom was it made?

4. What is the lowest score made by Pakistan in a Test Match? Against whom was it made?

5. Pakistan plays Tests against five other countries. Which batsmen have scored centuries against all five?

6. Which two batsmen put up a record for the 9th wicket in Test cricket? How many did they score, and against whom?

7. Which batsman has made the highest score in first class cricket?

8. What is the highest number of wickets taken in a Test Match by a Pakistan bowler, and who was he?

9. What is the greatest number of dismissals in a Test by a Pakistan wicket-keeper? Who was he, and against whom did he perform that feat?

10. Two Pakistan bowlers have taken over 100 wickets in Tests. Names, please.

(Answers on Pages 44 and 45)

SOUTH AFRICA

1. South Africa has played Tests against three other countries, but only one batsman has scored a century against all three. Name, please.

2. Two South Africans have scored two centuries in the same Test match. Who are they?

3. Two South Africans have scored a double-century in a Test Match on two occasions. Who are they?

4. What is the lowest score made in an innings by a South African team in a Test Match, and against whom was it played?

5. What is the lowest score made against South Africa in a Test match innings, and which team made it?

6. What is the largest score made against South Africa in a Test Match, and who made it?

7. What is the greatest number of wickets taken by a South African bowler in one innings in a Test Match? Who took them, and against whom?

8. One South African has done the hat-trick in a Test Match. Who, and against whom?

9. What is the greatest number of victims in a Test series dismissed by a South African wicket-keeper? And who was he?

10. South African hold the unfortunate record of having amassed the lowest aggregate in a Test Match. What was the score in each innings, and against whom was South Africa playing?

(Answers on Page 45)

NEW ZEALAND

1. The greatest number of centuries scored in Tests by a New Zealand batsman is six. Who was the batsman, and against which countries did he score his centuries?

2. A New Zealand cricketer holds the record for the greatest number of 6's hit in an innings. Who was he, and how many 6's did he hit?

3. Three New Zealand batsmen have scored over 200 in a Test innings. Who are they, and against whom did they make the runs?

4. What is the highest score made by New Zealand in a Test, and against which country was it made?

5. What is the highest Test score made against New Zealand, and who made it?

6. What is the lowest score made against New Zealand in a Test, and who made it?

7. What is the greatest number of batsmen dismissed by a New Zealand wicket-keeper in a Test series, who was the wicket-keeper, and against whom did he perform that feat?

8. One New Zealand batsman has scored 3000 runs in Tests. Who is he?

9. What is the lowest total for an innings made in a Test Match by New Zealand?

10. What is the highest individual score made in first class cricket by a New Zealand batsman, and who was he?

(Answers on Page 46)

NOT SO WELL KNOWN

1. Where is the Fenner Knock-out Competition staged?

2. How many cricket Leagues are there in Lancashire, and what are their names?

3. How many cricket Leagues are there in Scotland, and what are their names?

4. Where is the Guiness Cup competed for, and how many teams compete? What are their names?

5. Where is the Rothman Quaich competed for?

6. Who captained England in the Test series against Australia played in England in 1976?

7. Which cricket club fields both men's teams and women's teams?

8. In what competition does a combined Oxford and Cambridge team play?

9. Which countries belong to the International Cricket Conference?

10. What matches, played in Great Britain, are 'first-class matches'?

(Answers on Pages 46 and 47)

ANSWERS TO QUESTION ON PAGE 7

1. Eleven.
2. Three stumps and two bails. But if there is a very high wind the captains and umpires may agree to play without the bails.
3. Twenty-two yards, measured from one wicket to the other.
4. Twenty-eight inches above ground.
5. Not more than four and a quarter inches—slightly less than half the width of the wicket, which is nine inches.
6. (a) The bowling crease is in line with the stumps. (b) The popping crease is four feet in front of the bowling crease. (c) the return creases (there are two of them) are at right angles to the bowling crease and run backwards from the wicket.
7. At the start of each innings, and at the start of each day's play.
8. A cube of cork with worsted wound round it, enclosed in leather dyed red.
9. Yes. If a ball is lost or unfit for play, another may be substituted, but it must have been used as often as the one it replaces.
10. They are all made in Kent, and by two firms: Alfred Reader & Co. at Teston, and John Wisden & Co. at Penshurst.

ANSWERS TO QUESTIONS ON PAGE 8

1. Each time batsmen cross, and pass the popping creases at the far end, one run is scored. If the ball touches or crosses the boundary, four runs are scored. If a hit pitches over the boundary, six runs are scored.
2. A run scored when a fieldsman throws in the ball but neither the bowler nor the wicket-keeper is able to catch it and the batsmen are able to cross.
3. (a) For changing his way of bowling without warning the batsman (changing from overarm to underarm, or from right-handed to left-handed). (b) For throwing the ball instead of bowling it. (c) If, when he delivers the ball, no part of his front foot is behind the popping crease or his back foot has not landed within the return creases.

4. If the ball passes a batsman without touching him, or touching his bat, and the umpire has not called 'Wide' or 'No-ball', the batsman may run. Any run so scored is called a 'bye'.
5. (a) By extending one arm horizontally. (b) By waving one hand from side to side. (The umpire signals '6' by raising both arms above his head.)
6. Yes. He can be run out.
7. When, after it has been bowled, it is (a) in the wicket-keeper's hands; (b) back in the bowler's hands; (c) at or over the boundary; (d) a batsman has been given out; (e) the umpire has called 'Over' or 'Time'; (f) the ball has become lodged in the batsman's pads or clothing.
8. (a) By extending both arms horizontally. (b) By raising one knee and tapping it with his hand.
9. If, at the end of the match, the side batting last has not finished its innings, and has not equalled or passed the total number of runs scored by the opposing side, the result is a draw. If the side batting last has finished its innings, and the scores of the two sides are equal, the result is a tie.
10. When the side batting last passes its opponent's total with some wickets still to fall, the result can be expressed as a win by the number of wickets still remaining. i.e. 'Surrey won by five wickets'.

ANSWERS TO QUESTIONS ON PAGE 9

1. Taking wickets in three successive deliveries. For performing this feat, a bowler was once rewarded with the present of a top-hat. (The first recorded instance of this was in 1858.)
2. (a) Delivering the ball, when bowling, from the hand furthest away from the stumps; (b) delivering the ball from the hand nearer the stumps. i.e. a bowler, bowling '*round the wicket*', bowls from the right of the wicket if he is right-handed, and from the left if he is a left-hander.
3. An off-break bowled with a leg-break action. It was discovered by B. J. T. Bosanquet (Middlesex and England) and was once called a 'Bosie'.
4. A ball that arrives without bouncing. A full toss from a fieldsman arrives in the wicket-keeper's gloves without bouncing; to a batsman, a full toss arrives on his bat without bouncing.

5. Runs scored from no-balls, wides, byes and leg-byes.
6. The right side. (The left side is called the 'on'.)
7. An over from which no runs are scored by the batsman.
8. If the side batting in a three or four day match bowls out the other side while it is still 150 or more runs behind, it may ask that side to begin its second innings at once. This is called asking the side to 'follow-on'. In a two day match, a lead of only 100 runs is required; in a match of five days or more, a lead of 200 runs is required.
9. A batsman who scores very slowly. (Playing for England against South Africa, T. E. Bailey once scored eight runs in two hours. This was a good bit of stonewalling.)
10. A ball bowled, or thrown, underhand. (In 1909 G. H. Simpson-Hayward bowled lobs in a Test Match against South Africa—and took 6 for 43!)

ANSWERS TO QUESTIONS ON PAGE 10

1. Seventeen.
2. Yorkshire have won the title outright thirty-one times, and shared it twice.
3. Surrey, in 1952–58. (Nottingham shared the title in 1879, won it in 1880, shared it in 1882, and won it in 1883–86, after which Surrey won in 1887 and 1888, shared it in 1889, and won in 1890–92.)
4. Cambridgeshire played in the Championship in 1864–69 and in 1871, and then dropped out.
5. In 1920 P. G. H. (Percy) Fender, playing for Surrey against Northamptonshire, scored 100 in thirty-five minutes. He and H. A. Peach scored 171 together in forty-two minutes.
6. Glamorgan joined in 1921.
7. Leicestershire, captained by R. (Ray) Illingworth, won the Championship in 1975, ninety-six years after the County Club had been formed.
8. (a) Ten points for a win, plus bonus points for batting and bowling awarded in the first innings; (b) Five points for a tie, plus bonus points for batting and bowling awarded in the first innings. (c) If scores are equal in a drawn game, the side batting in the fourth innings receives five points, plus bonus points.
9. One point for scoring 150–199 runs; two for 200–249; three for 250–299; four for over 300 runs in 100 overs.

10. One point for 3–4 wickets taken; two for 5–6 wickets; three for 7–8 wickets; four for 9–10 wickets.

ANSWERS TO QUESTIONS ON PAGE 11

1. Sixty.
2. Two. East and West.
3. England, Australia, West Indies, India, Pakistan, New Zealand, Sri Lanka, East Africa.
4. (a) Not more than twelve. (b) Not more than eight. (c) Not more than eleven.
5. The West Indies beat Australia in the final by 17 runs.
6. Nineteen. (By D. B. (Brian) Close (Somerset) in 1974, and J. A. Jameson (Warwickshire) in 1975.)
7. Forty-one. (Scored by Cambridgeshire—off 20 overs; Middlesex—off 19.4 overs; and Shropshire—off 36.1 overs.)
8. 327 for 4 off 55 overs. Scored by Leicestershire against Warwickshire, 1972.
9. 155 not out. By B. A. (Barry) Richards (Hampshire).
10. 7 for 15. By A. L. Dixon (Kent) against Surrey in 1967.

ANSWERS TO QUESTIONS ON PAGE 12

1. 36. Scored by G. S. (Gary) Sobers playing for Nottinghamshire against Glamorgan in 1968. The unfortunate bowler was M. A. Nash.
2. 887. Scored by Yorkshire against Warwickshire in 1896.
3. 12. Scored by Northamptonshire against Gloucestershire in 1907.
4. 424. Scored by A. C. McLaren (Lancashire) against Somerset in 1895.
5. 100.12. by G. (Geoff) Boycott (Yorkshire) in 1971. The first time an Englishman had had an average of over 100.
6. W. R. (Wally) Hammond (Gloucestershire) held ten catches in the game against Surrey in 1928. That season he caught seventy-eight.

7. 555. Made by H. Sutcliffe (313) and P. Holmes (224 not out) for Yorkshire against Essex in 1932. Yorkshire declared when Sutcliffe was out, and Essex lost by an innings and 313 runs.
8. 304. By A. P. Freeman (Kent) in 1928.
9. 18. By D. E. S. (Dennis) Compton) in 1947.
10. 11. By A. Long (Surrey) in the game against Sussex in 1964.

ANSWERS TO QUESTIONS ON PAGE 13

1. In alphabetical order they are: J. J. Ferris (Australia); F. Hearne (England) who later played for South Africa; W. E. Midwinter (Australia); F. Mitchell (England) who later played for South Africa; W. L. Murdoch (Australia); the Nawab of Pataudi (India); A. E. Trott (Australia); S. M. J. Woods (Australia).
2. H. G. Owen-Smith played for South Africa against England in 1929 and scored a century. He played at fullback for the England XV.
3. 26. By New Zealand against England in 1955.
4. Cambridge University against the West Indies in 1950. For Cambridge, who batted first, Dawes and Sheppard scored 343 for the first wicket, and declared at 595 for 4. For the West Indies, Worrel and Weekes put on 350 together, Weekes scored 304 not out, and the score reached 730 for 3.
5. (a) At Kingston, Jamaica, in 1930. England scored 849 in the first innings, and the West Indies, who needed 836 to win, reached 408 for 5 in their second innings. (George Headley 223.) (b) At Durban, South Africa, in 1939. England were left to score 696 in the fourth innings and reached 645 for 5.
6. In the Oxford v Cambridge match in 1870 Oxford, with seven wickets down, needed only three runs to win. F. C. Cobden then did the hat-trick and Cambridge won.
7. In 1963 J. T. Murray scored 3 not out against Australia in 100 minutes. He was the wicket-keeper and had badly damaged a shoulder making a brilliant catch in the Australian innings. A deliberately slow innings was that of T. E. Bailey for England against South Africa in 1955. He scored 8 in two hours.

ANSWERS TO QUESTIONS ON PAGE 14

1. R. G. Pollock and P. M. Pollock. R. G. scored 517 runs for an average of 73.85; P. M. took 15 wickets for 17.2 runs each.
2. G. Gunn and his son G. V. Gunn, playing for Nottinghamshire against Warwickshire. G. scored 183 and G. V. 100 not out.
3. In 1889, playing for Worcestershire against Hampshire, W. L. Foster scored 140 and 172 not out; R. E. Foster scored 134 and 101 not out.
4. G. S. Sobers and D. A. J. Holford, playing for the West Indies, put on 274 against England without being parted: This is a record for Tests between England and the West Indies. (The West Indian record for the sixth wicket is 487, scored in a match in 1932 between Jamaica and an English XI captained by Lord Tennyson.)
5. W. G. Grace, E. M. Grace and G. F. Grace played for England against Australia in 1880. W. G. Grace scored 152, the first Test century scored by an Englishman. G. F. Grace scored 0 and 0, and was the first batsman to get 'a pair of spectacles' in a Test.
6. J. W. Lee and F. S. Lee—in 1934.
7. Seven. The Foster brothers: R. E., G. N., H. K., M. K., N. J. A., W. L., and B. S. At one time the county was called 'Fostershire' instead of Worcestershire!
8. Wazir Mohammad, Hanif Mohammad, Mushtaq Mohammad and Sadiq Mohammad. Hanif, Mushtaq and Sadiq were in the Pakistan team in the first Test against New Zealand in 1969. Mushtaq and Sadiq played in all four Tests against England in 1971.
9. G. S. and I. M. Chappel (Australia) against England at the Oval. G. S. scored 113 and I. M. scored 118.
10. In 1862 E. M. Grace scored 192 and took 10 wickets for 69. His brother W. G. scored 104 and took 10 for 49 in 1886.

ANSWERS TO QUESTIONS ON PAGE 15

1. Denmark, Holland, Gibraltar and Corfu.

2. Sri Lanka, Malaysia, Singapore, Hong Kong, Bangladesh, and Thailand.
3. (a) For the winners of the competition between Jamaica, Barbados, Trinidad, Guyana and Combined Islands (West Indies) (b) For the winner of the competition between the New Zealand provinces (c) For the winners of a Test series between England and the West Indies (d) For the scorer of the fastest century in the English County Championship.
4. The West Indies.
5. (a) Kingston, Jamaica (b) Cambridge, England (c) Wellington, New Zealand.
6. (a) K. S. Ranjitsinhji: 154 not out at Manchester in 1896 (b) K. S. Duleepsinhji: 173 at Lords in 1930 (c) The Nawab of Pataudi: 102 at Sydney, Australia, in 1932–3.
7. G. S. Sobers has scored the greatest number of runs, and L. R. Gibbs has taken most wickets in Tests. Both played for the West Indies.
8. (a) The greatest number of runs in a day in Tests is 503 for 2 by England against South Africa in 1924. (b) The lowest score in a day in Tests is Australia 80, Pakistan 15 for 2 in Pakistan in 1956.
9. Australia won by 45 runs in both Tests.
10. England was captained by A. W. (Tony) Greig, and Australia by G. S. Chappell. The game was played at Melbourne, Australia, where the 1877 game had been played.

ANSWERS TO QUESTIONS ON PAGE 16

1. G. M. Turner (New Zealand and Worcestershire). He scored 1018 for the New Zealand touring team in 1973.
2. 628 not out, by A. E. J. Collins in a House Match at Clifton.
3. C. L. Townsend (Gloucestershire) in a game against Somerset. The wicket-keeper was W. H. Brain.
4. W. J. Stewart, playing for Warwickshire against Lancashire, hit 10 sixes in his first innings of 155, and 7 sixes in his second innings of 125, a total of 17 sixes.
5. L. Hutton (Yorkshire and England) scored 364 against Australia at the Oval in 1938.

6. J. C. Laker (Surrey and England) took 19 wickets in a Test against Australia in 1956. He took 10 for 53 and 9 for 37, a total of 19 for 90.
7. In 1956 Lancashire beat Leicestershire by 10 wickets at Manchester. Lancashire declared at 166 for 0 in the first innings, and scored 66 for 0 in the second.
8. 238 not out by the Nawab of Pataudi (Oxford). In the same match, in 1931, A. Ratcliffe made 201 for Cambridge.
9. 32, by Oxford in 1878.

ANSWERS TO QUESTIONS ON PAGE 17

1. Sir Donald Bradman (b. 1908). In 80 Test innings he made 6996 runs, an average of 99.9.
2. W. G. Grace (1848–1915) made 318 not out for Gloucestershire against Yorkshire in 1876, and took 17 Notts wickets for 89 in 1877.
3. F. R. Spofforth (1853–1926) took 14 for 90 against England at the Oval in 1882, and in 18 Tests took 94 wickets.
4. F. S. Trueman (b. 1931). Yorkshire and England. In 67 Tests, he took 307 wickets and is the only fast bowler to have taken 300 wickets in Test cricket.
5. W. J. O'Reilly (b. 1905). New South Wales and Australia. He took 144 wickets in 27 Tests, and 102 wickets against England. With Bradman he put on 78 for the ninth wicket against South Africa in 1931–2.
6. F. H. Tyson (b. 1930). Northamptonshire. He took 32 wickets in only 8 Tests against Australia. In 1954 he took 10 for 130 in the second Test in Australia and 9 for 95 in the third.

ANSWERS TO QUESTIONS ON PAGE 18

1. G. T. S. Stevens (1901–70). He scored 466 in a House Match while at University College School.
2. 499 by Hanif Mohammad (Pakistan).
3. (a) Australia: D. G. Bradman—452 (1929–30) (b) India: B. B. Nimbalkar—443 (1948–9) (c) New Zealand: B. Sutcliffe—385 (1952–3) (d) West Indies: G. S. Sobers—365 (1957–8).
4. W. G. Grace and F. E. Woolley.

5. J. B. Hobbs (Surrey and England. 1882–1963).
6. 345 by C. G. Macartney (Australia) in 1921 against Nottinghamshire.
7. D. E. S. Compton (3816) and W. J. Edrich (3539) both of Middlesex.
8. 1107 by Victoria against New South Wales in 1926–7.
9. W. R. Hammond (Gloucestershire and England) scored 50,493 runs and made 167 centuries.
10. M. C. (Colin) Cowdrey. 307 against South Australia in 1962–3.

ANSWERS TO QUESTIONS ON PAGE 19

1. J. Laker (Surrey) took all 10 Australian wickets in 1956 for Surrey against the Australians at the Oval. In the same year, playing for England against Australia at Manchester, he took all 10 wickets again.
2. A. E. Trott (Middlesex) playing against Somerset at Lords in 1907.
3. H. Verity (Yorkshire) took 10 for 10 against Nottinghamshire in 1932; 9 for 12 against Kent in 1936; 7 for 9 against Sussex in 1939.
4. W. Rhodes (Yorkshire) took 4187 wickets (127 in Tests).
5. F. S. Trueman (Yorkshire); D. L. Underwood (Kent); J. B. Statham (Lancashire).
6. L. R. Gibbs and G. S. Sobers.
7. R. Benaud; G. D. McKenzie; R. R. Lindwall and C. V. Grimmett.
8. R. C. Motz and B. R. Taylor.
9. Fazal Mahmood and Intikhab Alam.
10. T. J. Matthews. The Test Match between Australia and South Africa was played in England in 1912. Matthews did the hat-trick in the New Zealand's first innings, and, when they followed-on, he did it again.

ANSWERS TO QUESTIONS ON PAGE 20

1. 'The double' is the feat of scoring 1000 runs and taking 100 wickets in one season. It was last performed by F. J. Titmus (Middlesex) in 1967.

2. W. Rhodes (Yorkshire) did the double on 16 occasions.
3. W. Rhodes (Yorkshire) in the 1903–4 season helped R. E. Foster to put on 130 for the last wicket against Australia. In 1911–12 Rhodes and J. B. Hobbs (Surrey) scored 323 for the first wicket against Australia.
4. R. Benaud scored 2201 runs and took 248 wickets.
5. V. Mankad with P. Roy scored 413 for the first wicket for India against New Zealand in 1955–6. In 1951–2 Mankad took 8 for 55 against England, and in 1952–3 he took 8 for 52 against Pakistan.
6. F. J. (Fred) Titmus.
7. T. L. Goddard scored 2516 runs in Test cricket and took 123 wickets.
8. C. B. Fry (1872–1956). He also scored two separate hundreds in the same match five times, and in 1901 he made over 100 in each of six successive innings.

ANSWERS TO QUESTIONS ON PAGE 21

1. C. Washbrook (Lancashire) with L. Hutton made 359 for the first wicket for England against South Africa in 1948–9. In 1946–7 against Australia they scored over 100 in three successive innings.
2. W. M. Lawry (Victoria) in 1964–5 made 382 with R. B. Simpson against the West Indies, and in 1965–6 they made 244 together against England.
3. J. C. Laker. In 1956, playing for Surrey, Laker took all 10 wickets against Kent. In the Test in which Laker took 19 Australian wickets, Lock took the other one. Both have done the hat-trick four times.
4. R. R. Lindwall. Lindwall took 228 wickets in 61 Tests, and Miller 170 in 55 Tests. Miller scored 2958 runs, and Lindwall 1502.
5. A. L. Valentine. Valentine took 139 wickets in 36 Tests, Ramadhin 158 in 43 Tests. Both took 11 wickets in a Test, and both took part in a record West Indian Test partnership for the tenth wicket: Valentine against Australia (31 with W. W. Hall), and Ramadhin against England (55 with F. Worrell).

6. J. H. Edrich. In 1947 D. C. S. Compton made 3816 runs and Edrich made 3539.
7. H. Sutcliffe (Yorkshire). On twenty-six occasions J. B. Hobbs and H. Sutcliffe scored over 100 for the first wicket. In 1924–5 against Australia they made over 100 in three successive innings.
8. J. B. Statham (Lancashire). F. S. Trueman took 307 wickets in 67 Tests, and J. B. Statham 252 in 70 Tests. Trueman did the hat-trick four times, Statham three times.
9. W. Voce (Nottinghamshire). H. Larwood took 78 wickets in 21 Tests, and W. Voce 98 in 27 Tests.
10. J. R. Thomson. In the Test series in 1974–5, in Australia, Thomson took 33 wickets and Lillee took 25. In the Test series in 1975, in England, Thomson took 34 wickets, and Lillee took 41.

ANSWERS TO QUESTIONS ON PAGE 22

1. In the Pavilion at the Oval. It dates from 1729.
2. Lord Byron. (Eton won.)
3. Gentlemen v Players. The 'Gentlemen's' team was composed of amateurs, the 'Players' were professionals. In 1962 all became 'cricketers'.
4. Games between Eton and Harrow date from 1805. Games between Oxford and Cambridge from 1827.
5. Kent v England in 1744. A poem describing the match was published later in the same year.
6. M. C. Cowdrey scored 104 in the third Test against Australia in 1968. In the same innings he brought the number of runs he had scored in Test Matches to over 7000.
7. In 1814. The first ground called Lord's was opened in 1787 and the second in 1809. In each case the turf was transferred from one ground to the other.
8. In the first Test Match ever played, C. Bannerman went in first for Australia and scored 165 before having to retire hurt. The game was played at Melbourne in 1877 and Australia won by 45 runs.
9. Eton played Westminster without getting permission from the Headmaster.

ANSWERS TO QUESTIONS ON PAGE 23

1. The Ashes are a symbol of victory in a Test series between England and Australia. Their origin dates from 1882 when England were unexpectedly defeated by Australia and the '*Sporting Times*' published a notice of the death of English cricket, concluding with the words: 'The body will be cremated and the ashes taken to Australia'. In 1883 when England won the second and third Tests in Australia, a bail was burned and the ashes put in an urn and presented to the English captain. They are now at Lords. England retained them in 1972, but lost them in 1974–5.
2. In 1877 England and Australia played the first Test, which was won by Australia by 45 runs.
3. Australia; South Africa (up to 1965); West Indies; New Zealand; India; Pakistan.
4. In the England v Pakistan Test series in 1972–3 England were captained by A. R. Lewis and Pakistan by Majid J. Khan. Both Lewis and Majid captained Glamorgan.
5. S. F. Barnes took 49 wickets in 4 Tests against South Africa in 1913–14.
6. New Zealand. They beat Pakistan 1–0, with two games drawn, in 1969, and so won the series.
7. The West Indies and Australia tied the first Test at Brisbane in 1960. (When the last over began, Australia needed 6 to win and had 3 wickets in hand.)
8. (a) Australia (b) South Africa (c) Pakistan (d) West Indies (e) England (f) India.
9. Australia beat England 5–0 in 1920–21. Australia beat South Africa 5–0 in 1931–32. England beat India 5–0 in 1959. West Indies beat India 5–0 in 1961–2. (In 1969–70 South Africa won all 4 Tests against Australia.)
10. K. D. Walters (Australia)—242 and 103 against West Indies, 1968–9. S. M. Gavaskar (India)—124 and 220 against West Indies, 1970–1. L. G. Rowe (West Indies)—214 and 100 against New Zealand, 1971–2. G. S. Chappell (Australia)—247 and 133 against New Zealand, 1973–4.

ANSWERS TO QUESTIONS ON PAGE 24

1. In 1970–71 England were captained by R. Illingworth, and Australia by W. H. Lawry and I. M. Chappell.

2. T. W. Graveney captained England, and B. N. Jarman captained Australia in the fourth Test at Headingley (Leeds).
3. England were defeated by an innings and 332 runs at Brisbane in 1946 (Australia 645; England 141 and 172); Australia were defeated by an innings and 579 runs at the Oval in 1938 (England 903 for 7 declared; Australia 201 and 123).
4. In the fourth Test, at Old Trafford, England bowled out Australia for 86 in the second innings, and had to score only 124 to win. They were bowled out for 120 and Australia won by 3 runs. In the fifth Test, at the Oval, England had to make 263 to win and lost 5 wickets for 48. G. L. Jessop then scored 104 in 75 minutes, and England finally won by 1 wicket.
5. For England, J. B. Hobbs made 12 centuries and scored 3636 runs. For Australia D. G. Bradman made 19 centuries and scored 5028 runs.
6. In 1956, at Manchester, J. Laker took 19 wickets for 90 runs (9 for 37, and 10 for 53).
7. Seven. In 1938, at Nottingham, centuries were scored for England by E. Paynter (216 not out); C. J. Barnett (126), D. Compton (102), and L. Hutton (100). For Australia by S. J. McCabe (232), D. G. Bradman (144 not out), and W. A. Brown (133). The match was drawn.

ANSWERS TO QUESTIONS ON PAGE 25

1. C. L. Walcott (4 against England; 5 against Australia; 1 against New Zealand; 4 against India; 1 against Pakistan). E. D. Weekes (4 against England; 1 against Australia; 3 against New Zealand; 7 against India; 1 against Pakistan). G. S. Sobers (10 against England; 4 against Australia; 1 against New Zealand; 8 against India; 2 against Pakistan).
2. G. S. Sobers: 365 not out against Pakistan, 1957–8. L. G. Rowe: 302 against England, 1973–4.
3. A. M. E. Roberts against India, 1974–5.
4. 76 against Pakistan, 1958–9.
5. 74 by New Zealand, 1956.
6. In 1930 England scored 849 at Kingston, Jamaica. (The largest by the West Indies was 681 for 8 against England at Port of Spain in 1954.)

7. A. L. Valentine against England, 1950. L. R. Gibbs against India, 1961–2.
8. W. W. Hall against Pakistan, 1958–9. L. R. Gibbs against Australia, 1960–1.
9. In 1957 S. Ramadhin bowled 129 overs (774 balls) in the Test against England at Birmingham. In one innings he bowled 98 overs (588 balls) which is also a record.
10. In 1963, in Tests against England, D. L. Murray dismissed 24 batsmen—22 caught, 2 stumped.

ANSWERS TO QUESTIONS ON PAGE 26

1. V. S. Hazare scored 145 and 116 against Australia, 1947–8. S. M. Gavaskar scored 124 and 220 against the West Indies, 1970–71.
2. P. R. Umrigar. 223 against New Zealand, 1955–6. V. Mankad. 231 and 233 against New Zealand, 1955–6. Nawab of Pataudi. 203 not out against England, 1963–4. D. N. Sardesai. 200 not out against New Zealand, 1964–5.
3. In 1955–6 India scored 537 for 3 at Madras against New Zealand.
4. On two occasions India were bowled out for 58—by Australia at Brisbane in 1947, and by England at Manchester in 1952.
5. V. S. Hazare (288) and Gul Mohammed (319) put on 577 for the fourth wicket, playing for Baroda against Holkar.
6. V. Mankad (231) and P. Roy (173) put on 413 for the first wicket against New Zealand in 1955–6.
7. S. P. Gupte against the West Indies, 1958–9. J. M. Patel against Australia, 1959–60.
8. J. M. Patel took 14 for 124 against Australia at Kanpur, 1959–60.
9. A. W. Greig and B. S. Bedi.
10. P. R. Umrigar, V. L. Manjrekar and C. G. Borde.

ANSWERS TO QUESTIONS ON PAGE 27

1. Hanif Mohammad scored 3915 runs in Test cricket.
2. Hanif Mohammad (twice). 337 against West Indies, 203 against New Zealand; Imtiaz Ahmed. 209 against New

Zealand; Zahir Abbas (twice). 274 and 240, both against England; Mushtaq Mohammad. 201 against New Zealand.
3. 657 for 8 against West Indies, 1957–8.
4. 87 against England, 1954.
5. Hanif Mohammad and Mushtaq Mohammad. Hanif scored 3 against England, 3 against New Zealand, 2 against Australia, 2 against West Indies, and 2 against India. Mushtaq scored 3 against England, 1 against New Zealand, 1 against Australia, 1 against West Indies, and 1 against India.
6. Asif Iqbal and Intikhab Alam scored 190 for the ninth wicket against England at the Oval in 1967.
7. Hanif Mohammad scored 499 playing for Karachi against Bahawalpur, 1958–9.
8. 13 by Fazal Mahmood against Australia, 1956–7.
9. 8 (all caught) by Wasim Bari against England, 1971.
10. Fazal Mahmood and Intikhab Alam.

ANSWERS TO QUESTIONS ON PAGE 28

1. D. J. McGlew scored 2 centuries against England, 2 against Australia and 3 against New Zealand.
2. B. Mitchell against England, 1947; A. Melville against England, 1947.
3. A. D. Nourse scored 231 against Australia (1935–6) and 208 against England (1951). R. G. Pollock scored 209 (1966–7) and 274 (1970), both times against Australia.
4. 30. Twice South Africa were bowled out for 30, each time by England (1895 and 1924).
5. 75 by Australia in 1950.
6. 654 for 5 by England at Durban in 1939.
7. H. J. Tayfield took 9 for 113 against England in 1956.
8. G. M. Griffin against England, 1960. (In 1970 E. J. Barlow of South Africa, playing for the Rest of the World against England, took 4 wickets in 5 balls at Leeds.)
9. J. H. B. Waite in Tests against New Zealand in 1961–2 took 26 wickets—23 caught, 3 stumped.
10. At Melbourne, Australia, in 1931–2 South Africa were dismissed for 36 and 45. (Of the aggregate of 81, extras totalled 12.)

ANSWERS TO QUESTIONS ON PAGE 29

1. B. E. Congdon scored 3 centuries against England, 1 against Australia, and 2 against the West Indies.
2. J. R. Reid in 1962–3, playing for Wellington against Northern Districts, hit 15 sixes.
3. M. P. Donnelly made 206 against England at Lords, 1949. G. T. Dowling made 239 against India at Christchurch, New Zealand, 1967–8. B. Sutcliffe made 230 not out against India at New Delhi, 1955–6.
4. 505 at Cape Town against South Africa, 1953–4.
5. 561 at Lahore by Pakistan, 1955–6.
6. 77 at Auckland by West Indies, 1955–6.
7. 23—21 caught, 2 stumped—by A. E. Dick in 1961–2 in matches against South Africa.
8. J. R. Reid scored 3431 runs in 58 Tests.
9. 26 against England in 1954–5.
10. B. Sutcliffe scored 385 for Otago against Canterbury in 1952–3. (In 1949–50 he had scored 355 for Otago against Auckland, and in 1931–2 R. C. Blunt, also of Otago, had made 338 not out against Canterbury.)

ANSWERS TO QUESTIONS ON PAGE 30

1. Scarborough.
2. Two. The Lancashire League, and the Central Lancashire League.
3. Six. (a) Scottish Counties (b) Border League (c) Western Union (d) East League (e) Strathmore Union (f5 Glasgow and District League.
4. Ireland. Six teams compete. North-West, North Leinster, South Leinster, Ulster Country, Ulster Town, Munster.
5. Scotland.
6. Rachael Flint. The Tests were between women's teams.
7. Warwick District C.C., Western Australia.
8. The Benson and Hedges Cup Competition.
9. England, Australia, New Zealand, India, West Indies and Pakistan are full members. U.S.A., Sri Lanka, Fiji, Bermuda, Holland, Denmark, East Africa, Malaysia, Canada, Gibraltar, Hong Kong, Papua, New Guinea, Singapore, Israel, Argentina, West Africa, and Bangladesh are associate members.

10. (a) Games of three days or more against full members of the International Cricket Conference. (b) Games in the County Championship. (c) M.C.C. v teams in the County Championship. (d) Oxford v Cambridge. (e) Teams in the County Championship v Oxford or Cambridge. (f) Scotland v Ireland.